SAMUEL

Book 2

A CHILD'S BIBLE KIDS

Katheryn Maddox Haddad

Northern Lights Publishing House

Cover design by Sharon Lavy &
Jim Pagett, Images licensed by
Sweet Publishing http://sweetpublishing.com

Copyright © 2017 Katheryn Maddox Haddad

ISBN-978-1-948462-01-3

All rights reserved, including the right to reproduce this book or portions thereof in any form.
No part of this book may be reproduced, stored, transmitted, or distributed in any form or by any means
without prior written permission from the author.
The only exception is for a brief quotation in a printed review.

Printed in the United States.

NOTE: The author used mostly one-syllable words. Longer words were
sometimes hyphenated to help the child pronounce them.

Other Books By this Author For All Ages

HISTORICAL NOVELS
Series of 8: They Met Jesus
Ongoing Series of 8: Intrepid Men of God
Mysteries of the Empire with Klaudius & Hektor
Christmas: They Rocked the Cradle that Rocked the World
Series of 8: A Child's Life of Christ
Series of 10: A Child's Bible Heroes
Series of 8: A Child's Bible Kids
Series of 10: A Child's Bible Ladies

HISTORICAL RESEARCH BIBLE
for Novel, Screenwriter, Documentary & Thesis Writers

TOPICAL
Applied Christianity: Handbook 500 Good Works
Christianity or Islam? The Contrast
The Holy Spirit: 592 Verses Examined-
The Road to Heaven
Inside the Hearts of Bible Women-Reader+Audio+Leader
Revelation: A Love Letter From God
Worship Changes Since 1st Century + Worship 1sr Century Way
Was Jesus God? (Why Evil)
365 Life-Changing Scriptures Day by Date
The Road to Heaven
The Lord's Supper: 52 Readings with Prayers

FUN BOOKS
Bible Puzzles, Bible Song Book, Bible Numbers

TOUCHING GOD SERIES
365 Golden Bible Thoughts: God's Heart to Yours
365 Pearls of Wisdom: God's Soul to Yours
365 Silver-Winged Prayers: Your Spirit to God's

SURVEY SERIES: EASY BIBLE WORKBOOKS
→Old Testament & New Testament Surveys
→Questions You Have Asked-Part I & II

Genealogy: How to Climb Your Family Tree Without Falling Out
Volume I & 2: Beginner-Intermediate & Colonial-Medieval

Table of Contents

Other Books By this Author For All Ages iii

1 ~ Wishing 1
2 ~ Laughter 8
3 ~ A Happy Baby 15
4 – Playing With Toes 22
5 ~ Ride to the Temple 29
6 ~ The Grandfather 36
7 ~ New Home 44
8 ~ 10 Com-mand-ments 52
9 ~ A Priest 60
10 ~ The Voice 67

Thank You 77
Buy Your Next Child's Book Now 78

About the Author 79
Connect with the Author 80

Get a Free Book 81
Join My Dream Team 81

1 ~ Wishing

Samu-el wasn't even born yet. It took a very long time for him to get born.

If his mama had had her way, he would have been 20 years old by now. But she hadn't and he wasn't.

What was wrong with the world anyway? Hannah knew all along she would make a good mother. She had all these plans:

(1) Play with her baby everrrry day.

(2) Sing to her baby everrrry day.

(3) Feed her baby everrrry day.

(4) Uh, well, you get the idea...

So, here Hannah was—the perfect mama for the perfect baby.

She got married when she was 16 and told everyone she would have her first baby when she was 17.

She didn't.

So, when she was 26, she told

Book 2: Samuel

everyone she would have her first baby when she was 27.

She didn't.

So, when she was 36, she told everyone she would have her first baby when she was 37.

She didn't.

Sometimes Hannah would practice being a mama anyway. She would sit and fold her arms around a pretend baby and rock back and forth, back and forth.

And Hannah would sing to her baby who wasn't even born yet. Oh, how she loved to sing. She was so good at singing that sometimes she made up her own lullabies.

*Hush my little baby boy.
I will give you a tiny toy.*

Some people told Mama Hannah who wasn't really a mama yet that she ought to pray more.

Pray more? Pray more?

Hanna prayed when she first got up. She prayed when she put on her clothes for the day. She prayed when she fixed breakfast. She prayed when she ate breakfast.

She prayed prob-ably 50 times in a day. Some said she prayed 100 times a

Book 2: Samuel

day.

Day after day. Week after week. Year after year. Hannah prayed and prayed.

Didn't God hear prayers?

Hannah used to laugh a lot when she was young. But now she was starting to get a few gray hairs. And she was starting to cry more and more.

"I just do not understand God," she would say to her husband. "All the prophets say God answers prayers. Why doesn't God answer my prayers?"

Wow! Oh, wow!

A Child's Kids in the Bible

Dear reader. I have a big secret for you.

It took God a long time to give Hannah her baby because her baby was going to be so special.

Yes, indeedee. God had a great big and wonderful surprise just for Hannah.

I wonder what that sur-prise could be... Can you guess?

Book 2: Samuel

THINK & DO

1. Have you prayed for something for a very long time and never got it? Sometimes God just wants to see how badly you want that thing. Sometimes God wants you to wait so you can enjoy that thing more when you are older.

I know people who have prayed the same prayer for 20, 30, and 40 years. Then, when God finally gave them what they asked for, it was extra, extra special.

Stop right now and ask God again for that special something you want. Then decide you are going to keep praying for it until you are grown. Can you do that?

2 ~ Laughter

One time every year, Hannah and her husband went to the first capital city of the Israel-ites—Shiloh. The walls around the city were as high as 4 or 5 papas.

At Shiloh was a hill and on the hill was a special tent temple. Everyone went there to worship God at the special yearly feast.

One reason the tent temple was

Book 2: Samuel

special is the high priest over all the Israel-ites served God there. He was so important, all the other priests had to do whatever the high priest told them to.

This high priest's name was Eli. Eli's name meant "I belong to God."

Hannah was so pretty, the other women who went to the once-a-year feast wanted to look like her.

But it did not matter to Hannah what she looked like. She didn't care if she was a pretty or ugly mamma. She didn't care if she was a tall or short mama. She didn't care what she looked like. All she wanted to be was a mama.

Well, the special feast at the tent temple was over and everyone was ready to return home.

Hannah wanted to say one last prayer before she left. As she got closer to the tent temple, she got sadder and sadder. She began to cry.

She sobbed and sobbed and cried out loud. She could not stop the tears. Why couldn't she be happy again?

Little did she know God was about to do something special for her.

High Priest Eli was sitting on a seat by the entrance into the tent temple,

Book 2: Samuel

but Hannah did not notice him.

High Priest Eli watched the park across from the temple as Hannah sat on the ground looking up at the tent temple. He watched as she rocked back and forth, back and forth.

She began singing a lullaby in her mind. Her lips moved, but the melody was in her heart. It was a silent lullaby.

Finally, she told God, "If you will give me a baby boy, I will give him back to you so he will serve in your tent temple his whole life."

She said these words on the inside.

No one on the outside of her body could hear her.

High Priest Eli watched her and got mad. "She's drunk!" he said. "How dare she come to worship while she is drunk with wine!"

He walked over to Hannah. "You! You must leave. You are drunk. Go away!"

Did Hannah get up and run away? No.

Hannah looked up at High Priest Eli. "No! I am not drunk. I am just begging God to give me a baby."

Book 2: Samuel

Just then, High Priest Eli understood. He wasn't mad any more. Instead, he smiled.

"Well, then, you shall have your wish," the high priest said.

"Really?" Hannah replied.

Eli laughed out of happiness. Hannah laughed out of happiness. Even God in heaven laughed out of happiness.

THINK & DO

1. Has anyone ever said you did something you did not do? The best way to act after they do is to be so good, others do not believe you did anything bad at all.

2. Do you know anyone who is sad all the time? You may not be able to make them happy again, but you can draw a pretty picture to give them and they will smile for you.

Book 2: Samuel

3 ~ A Happy Baby

All Hannah's friends and neigh-bors back at their home wondered why she was suddenly so happy. Many had never seen her smile before.

When she was 17 she smiled. When she was 27 she didn't smile so much. When she was 37 she quit smiling.

Finally, one day, a - guessed. "Are you going to have a baby?"

"Yes!" Hannah said. "I am going to have a baby. And it is going to be a boy."

"How do you know?" the neigh-bor asked.

"Because High Priest Eli told me so."

Indeed, it happened just as High Priest Eli had said it would. Hannah had her baby.

Now, Hannah no longer had to rock a pretend baby. Her baby was real. No longer did she have to sing to a pretend baby. Her baby was real.

Book 2: Samuel

"What is the baby's name?" everyone asked.

"Samu-el," Hannah said. "It means "gift of God."

Little Samu-el was a happy baby. If someone touched his tiny nose, he would wiggle it and giggle. If someone tickled his toes, he would kick and giggle.

Then baby Samu-el wasn't a baby any more. He had learned to walk. He would pad around the house and giggle. If his mother took him on a picnic, he would pad around on the grass and the grass would make his little feet tickle.

Then Samu-el learned to talk. He

couldn't say as many words and you and I, but he could say mama and papa and milk and other simple words.

Hannah began to teach him to pray. She would kneel beside his little bed at night and Samu-el would too.

"Dear God," she would say, and he would say the same thing. "Thank you for my nose and toes," she would say, and he would say the same thing.

"Help me be a good boy," she would say. Then Samu-el would giggle.

"Oh, Mama, you are not a boy. You're a girl!"

They both would giggle and think

Book 2: Samuel

maybe God giggled a little too. Then they would become seri-ous again.

Samu-el had a papa too, of course.

When his papa came home from work every night, Samu-el would sit on his knee and be bounced.

They had such a happy family now. Everyone was happy.

But one day, Samu-el's papa saw Hannah crying.

"Why are you crying, Sweet-heart?" he asked.

"Because I promised God I would give my baby boy back to him if I could have him at home for just a little while."

"We have had a happy 2 years with him, haven't we?" he said.

"Yes. I must now help him understand he has to go away."

Book 2: Samuel

THINK & DO

1. Do you have a baby brother or sister? Sometimes it cries. What are some reasons babies cry?

When you feed or change or do whatever the baby needs, it stops crying. Then does your baby smile? What do you do to make your baby smile?

2. If you do not have a baby brother or sister, do you know anyone with a baby in your neigh-bor-hood or among your friends? Draw a picture of a baby. If you can write, say on your picture, "God loves babies."

4 ~ Playing With Toes

"Samu-el," Hannah said one day to her son who had just had his 3rd birthday. "We are going to have a little talk."

"That's silly, Mama," Samu-el said. "We talk all the time."

Hannah smiled. "Yes, we do. But this time we are going to talk about something very seri-ous."

Book 2: Samuel

"Do I have to put on a grumpy face to talk ser...ser... what-ever that word was?" Samu-el asked.

"No, of course not. We can talk seri-ous and still smile. Shall we agree to smile when we talk seri-ous?"

"Okay, Mama. I am smiling now, so we can talk ser...ser...you know."

Hannah drew Samu-el close and set him on her lap.

"We are going to go on a little trip."

"Oh, goodie," Samu-el said. "I like trips. Where to?"

"We're going to a place called Shiloh. Can you say Shiloh, Samu-el? It sounds like high-low, but starts with Sh instead of H."

Samu-el jumped down off his mother's lap. "Uh course, I can: Shi-loh," he said grinning.

"Very good, Samu-el. Now come back up here and sit on my lap. I need to tell you what is going to happen at Shiloh."

Samu-el climbed up onto his mother's lap. "It is ser…ser…?"

"Yes, this is the seri-ous part."

Hannah pressed her lips together,

took a deep breath, and tried to be brave.

"Our temple to God is a tent and it is at Shiloh. It is the most important and biggest city in the land." Her eyes got teary.

Samu-el pulled his feet up into his mother's lap and played with his toes.

"Samu-el, my sweet little boy," Hannah continued, "at the tent temple is the most important man in the land. He is our high priest. His name is Eli."

The little boy kept playing with his toes.

"He knows," Hannah thought to

herself. "I don't understand how he knows, but I think he does." She sighed.

"Samu-el, my sweet little boy," Eli is going to become your grandfather."

"No," Samu-el said, staring at his toes. "I don't want a grandfather. I want you and my Papa."

Hannah prayed silently for courage to say and do what she had promised God a long time ago she would say and do.

"Samu-el, your new grandfather is going to teach you how to be a kind of priest."

Book 2: Samuel

"I don't want to be a priest. What's a priest?"

"A priest is someone who serves God day and night."

"Doesn't a priest get to sleep?" Samu-el asked as he finally looked up in his mother's eyes.

Hannah smiled. "Yes, of course. I meant that he serves God when the sun is out and sometimes when the moon is out."

"Is my new grandfather nice?" Samu-el asked.

THINK & DO

1. Do you have a pretend grandfather or grandmother? Maybe they are old people who live in your neighborhood or go to church where you do.

Ask your mother to put a cookie in a baggie so you can take it to your pretend grandfather or grandmother. When you hand it to them, tell them, "You're just like my grandpapa" or "You're just like my grandmama."

You will make them smile.

Book 2: Samuel

5 ~ Ride to the Temple

The following morning, Samu-el's mama, Samu-el's papa, and Samu-el himself walked out of the only home Samu-el had ever known.

Samu'el's papa lifted Hannah up onto a wagon. He set little Samu-el in the seat beside his mother. Inside the wagon was a large bushel basket of flour. Tied to the back of the wagon was a donkey.

Samu-el's papa climbed onto the wagon and sat on the other side of Samu-el. He took the reins, snapped a whip in the air, and the 3 oxen pulling the wagon stepped forward.

The lazy oxen ambled on and on and on, never in a hurry.

Sometimes the little family stopped at a well beside the road for water. Sometimes they stopped and ate some cheese and grapes they had brought with them.

Then they would climb back onto the wagon and tell the oxen to go again.

Just as the sun began to turn red at the end of the day, they arrived at

Book 2: Samuel

Shiloh. The soldiers guarding the city closed the gate right after they got there.

Once inside, they looked up the high hill and saw the tent temple still in the same place where Hannah had prayed for a baby 3 years earlier.

That night, Samu-el's papa got a room at an inn for his family. They did not talk much. This made Samu-el play with his toes a lot. He was only 3, but he thought something seri-ous was going to happen soon. So, he kept playing with his toes.

The next day, the family got back in their wagon and went up the hill to the tent temple. His papa unhitched the 3 oxen and led them to the tent temple.

Hannah and Samu-el stayed where they were while Samu-el's papa went inside the temple court-yard where they had a large altar to cook things on that people called sac-ri-fices. Can you say that big word?

There was a park across from the entrance into the temple. As they waited there, Hannah reminded Samu-el of many things to remember that she had taught him. As she did, she tried to smile.

"Remember to always say your prayers. Pray when you get up in the morning, pray when the sun is high in

Book 2: Samuel

the sky, and pray before you go to bed. Okay?"

"Okay, Mama," Samu-el said.

"Remember the song we always sing when we're scared? If you get scared here, just sing that song. Okay?"

"Okay, Mama," Samu-el said.

"Remember, you get itchy when you eat olives. Remind your new grandfather if he ever gives you olives to eat. Okay?"

"Okay, Mama," Samu-el said.

After a while, Samu-el's papa came out of the temple to the park where his family had been waiting for him.

He had a bronze tray with him piled high with ox meat. There was bread with it made from the flour they had brought with them. He looked down at Hannah with sad eyes.

"It is done," he said. "I have ded-i-cated him to the Lord. He will spend the rest of his life here at the temple."

Hannah looked up at her husband. "Amen," she whispered. "So be it."

Book 2: Samuel

THINK & DO

1. I wonder what little 3-year-old Samu-el did on that trip to the tent temple that took all day. Do you have any ideas?

What types of things do you do on a long trip in the car or on a bus so you don't get bored?

2. Have you ever given up something you loved? Maybe you gave your favorite toy to a child with no toys. Maybe you gave your favorite shoes to someone with ragged shoes. Tell about it. If you haven't, what thing that you love will you give to someone who needs it?

6 ~ The Grandfather

In the days long ago when people offered sheep and oxen as sacri-fices to God, they didn't burn them up. They cooked them so they would have mutton and beef to eat. Eating their sacrifice was part of their worship.

Samu-el's papa sat down in the park with his family, brought out some bowls and divided the food among them.

"Samu-el," Hannah said, "would you

Book 2: Samuel

like to thank God for making us and giving us food and sunshine?"

Samu-el moved to his knees, folded his hands, bowed his head, and closed his eyes. "Thank you, God, for food and sunshine. Amen."

They ate slowly. Hannah did not eat much. She mostly watched her little Samu-el. She watched the way he licked his fingers when he ate greasy things. She watched how he wagged his head back and forth when his bites were too big and he got bored with chewing.

When he was done eating, Samu-el stood and looked up at the top of the temple. Then he turned in a circle with his arms out-stretched and hummed a tune his mother had taught him.

Hannah looked over at her husband and he nodded. She knew he meant it was time to go.

They put the rest of the meat in a basket and set it inside the wagon they had arrived in.

"It is time," Hannah said. "Yes, it is time," her husband said.

They stepped over to little Samuel, each took one of his chubby hands, and walked slowly to the entrance into the temple. As they did, an old man walked out. He was Eli, the high priest.

Book 2: Samuel

He smiled at them and would have passed them by because he did not recog-nize them. But Hannah stopped him.

"Uh, sir, I am the one you saw praying here 3 years ago. I told you I had promised, if God would give me a son, I would lend him to God the rest of his life."

Eli stared at Hannah, pulled on his gray beard, and nodded his head. "Yes, I do seem to remember that."

She let go of Samu-el's hand and kneeled next to him. She looked at her little boy, then up at High Priest Eli.

"This is that child. I have brought him to you."

She took hold of Samu-el's chubby hand again and stood. She looked into the eyes of the high priest, her own eyes misty.

"Teach him to serve God. Teach him to love God."

She took hold of Eli's old and gnarled hand, and put her son's in it.

"We told him you were going to be his new grandfather," Samu-el's papa said, putting Samu'el's other hand in Eli's.

Eli stooped so he would be eye-to-

Book 2: Samuel

eye with Samuel. He smiled. "You are such a fine young man," he said.

With that, the high priest picked up Samu-el in his arms and watched the boy's parents back away.

Hannah stopped. "Samu-el, my son," she called out, "God saves us from our enemies. Through you when you are grown, the people of our land will have no more enemies."

Samu-el watched his mother back away a little farther.

"The Lord makes fallen people alive, he makes the poor rich. He protects those who love him now and forever. Always remember that, my son."

With that, Samu-el's mama turned and hurried to the wagon. His papa had just finished hitching the donkey to it. The donkey pulled the wagon around and headed it down the hill.

Little Samu-el did not see them go. By now he was exploring the tent temple. But that night in his new little bed, he played with his toes. Then he prayed as his mama had told him to.

Book 2: Samuel

THINK & DO

1. It is hard to say good-bye to someone we love. Have you ever had to say good-bye to someone you love? Who was it?

Did you cry the rest of your life because that someone left? If you didn't, what made you smile again?

2. Do you know of a family with a grown son or daughter that is far away in the army defending our country's freedom? Tell the parents, "Thank you for sacri-ficing your son/daughter."

7 ~ New Home

It was morning. Samu-el's first morning of a strange new life away from his parents and now with a holy man.

He sat up in his little bed, looked around, and tried to remember where he was. His little hands formed knots and he brought them up to his misty eyes.

His mouth puck-ered, his little brow wrin-kled, his eyes closed half way, and

Book 2: Samuel

he began to cry. He kept looking around at the strange things around him.

He climbed out of his bed and headed for a doorway. He found himself in a hall in a strange building, and wandered down the hall, still crying.

"Mama? Mama? Where are you, Mama?" he mumbled between sobs. "Mama?"

He stopped and went the other way. "Mama? Mama? I can't find you, Mama."

He heard a voice. The voice was not of his mother. The voice was not of his papa. The voice was husky but friendly.

"Oh, there you are, my little priest," the voice said, gently taking Samu-el's fists down from his eyes and wiping a tear away.

The old man squatted so he could be eye-level with the boy. He smiled.

Samu-el stared at the old man with the long gray beard. "Grandfather?" he mumbled.

"Yes. That's right. I am your new grandfather," the old man replied.

High Priest Eli stood, took little Samu-el's hand, and walked up the hall.

"Where's my mama?" Samu-el asked looking up at the old man.

Book 2: Samuel

"She has gone back home."

"Can I go home?"

"This is your new home."

"But my mama isn't here. My papa isn't here."

High Priest Eli kept walking. He knew he had to show the little boy how to be brave, even though Samu-el was only 3 years old.

"You now have two homes. Your mama and papa will take care of your first home for you. I will person-ally take care of your new home for you. The Lord and I will both take care of your new home."

By this time, they had arrived in a court-yard of the big house.

"It is time to break our fast," Eli said. "Do you like grapes?"

Samu-el's eyes became bright and he managed a smile.

"Good. I like grapes too. So, we shall have grapes every morning."

Eli and Samu-el sat on fancy pillows on a fancier rug. As they ate, Eli began training Samu-el to be what he would be when he was all grown up.

"This is my house. I am giving you

Book 2: Samuel

the room you slept in last night. You will sleep there sometimes, and sometimes you will sleep in the temple to make sure the flames do not go out on the candle sticks. If they do, come get me."

As Samu-el ate, he looked around. Sometimes he reached down and played with his toes.

"As soon as you are through eating, we shall have a little-boy priest garment made for you."

"I'm not little. I'm 3," Samu-el replied.

THINK & DO

1. Was there ever a time you had to be very, very brave? Maybe a puppy died. But you had to finally stop crying. Maybe a family member moved away or you moved away. But you had to finally stop crying. Maybe you got hurt and couldn't walk. But you had to finally stop crying.

Share with the person reading this to you or with a friend what happened. Share how you decided to be brave and stop crying.

2. Sometimes after something bad happens, something new happens that makes you smile. Maybe you got a new puppy who could do tricks. Maybe you

Book 2: Samuel

got a new friend that was a lot of fun. Maybe you learned to do tricks when you couldn't walk for a while.

Draw a picture with a heart on it and give it to someone who became a special friend after your sad thing happened.

8 ~ 10 Commandments

Samu-el was now 6 years old. Every morning he went inside the temple with his little-boy broom and started sweeping. The morning went by slowly as little Samu-el was sweeping and sweeping and sweeping the whole temple area.

Noon time came. He stopped his work and went back to High Priest Eli's house next door to the temple.

Book 2: Samuel

"You are doing very well learning to read," Eli said, putting a piece of apple on Samu-el's plate. "You must know how to read so you can read the Laws God gave Moses for our people to keep."

"I can write my name," Samu-el said, just before taking a nibble out of his apple.

"Yes, you can, and I am proud of you," Eli said. "Someday you will be able to read and write the 10 Com-mand-ments all by yourself."

"I can count to 10," Samu-el said, popping a grape into his mouth. Then he counted to 10 for his grandfather.

Their meal was now over, it was

A Child's Kids in the Bible

time for Samu-el's daily lesson. High Priest Eli took Samu-el over to the park across from the door into the temple. They each had a rug that they spread out to sit on.

"Now, Samu-el," Eli said. "I am going to read to you the 10 Com-mand-ments and you tell me what they mean."

"I've got 10 toes," Samu-el said.

"Yes, you do," Eli said, "and you play with them when you get nervous. Now, here is Com-mand-ment #1: You shall believe in no pretend gods."

"Um," Samu-el said rolling his eyes up to stare at the clouds, "We must believe only in God who made us all."

Book 2: Samuel

"That's right," Eli responded. Here is Com-mand-ment #2. You shall not make statues to bow down to.

Samu-el stood up and swung in a circle. "We're not supposed to bow down to anything we can see. God is invis…invis…"

"God is invisible," Eli said. "Now for Com-mand-ment #3. You shall not use God's name as a swear word."

Samu-el turned a summersault. "We can only say God when we pray or talk about him."

"Very good. And Com-mand-ment #4. Keep the last day of the week holy."

Samu-el eased down on High Priest Eli's lap. "We can't sweep and other yucky things like that on a holy day."

Eli smiled and kissed Samu-el on the forehead. "And Com-mand-ment #5. Respect your father and mother."

Samu-el laid his head on Eli's chest. "When can I see my mama and papa? I want to hug and kiss and respect them."

"Very soon, Samu-el. Very soon. Now for Com-mand-ment #6. You shall not murder."

Samu-el stood, swung around, and stood on his head. "We can't throw

Book 2: Samuel

rocks at people we don't like and make them die."

"And Com-mand-ment #7. You shall not have a real wife plus a pretend wife."

"That's so silly, Grandfather," Samu-el said, wagging his head back and forth. "We can't have a wife and girlfriend at the same time."

"And Com-mand-ment #8. You shall not steal."

Samu-el plopped down onto his rug on his tummy and propped his head up with his hands. "We can't take something that someone else has."

"And Com-mand-ment #9. You shall not lie."

Samu-el sat up, legs crossed, and put his head down so far Eli could barely hear him. "Always tell the truth."

"And last, Com-mand-ment #10. You shall not let things or power be most impor-tant in your life."

Samu-el stood up, legs far apart, and thrust his fist up into the air. "God is most import… important! Yeah, I did it."

Book 2: Samuel

THINK & DO

1. Look again at the 10 Com-mand-ments in this story. If you can write, write them down on a piece of paper and put them on the wall somewhere in your house or apartment.

2. Try to memor-ize the 10 Com-mand-ments. Even though they are in the Bible, it is easier to say them from your mind wherever you are—at school, riding a bicycle, or going to sleep at night.

9 ~ A Priest

Samu-el was now 9 years old. As always, every morning he put on his long white robe, then wrapped a white strip of cloth around his waist and another strip around his head. Just like the priests.

He still swept the temple every day but could do it faster now. So, he also picked up the dirty priest clothes they took off after their duties at the altar and took them to be washed.

Book 2: Samuel

He also refilled the oil keeping the great candle-sticks in the temple lit. Their fire was never allowed to go out. Samu-el was proud of this new duty he was trusted with.

Today was going to be a special day. His mama and papa were coming to see him as they did every year.

At first, when they came to see Samu-el when he was 4 years old, he had trouble re-mem-bering what they looked like and who they were.

But the older he got, the easier it was to remember what they looked like. Grandfather Eli helped him.

Today, he rushed through his duties. Today was the special yearly feast. High Priest Eli was dressed in his special red, purple and blue robe with sparkling stones on his chest.

The city was always crowded on this special day for the yearly feast because all good Israel-ites in the land came to the feast if they could.

High Priest Eli brought in extra beds for Samu-el's room so his parents could sleep there.

As people came and went to the feast, Samu-el watched for his mama and papa.

"Samu-el. Samu-el," he finally

Book 2: Samuel

heard. "There you are." It was the voice of his mama.

Hannah rushed to her son and hugged him. Samu-el hugged her back. Then he hugged his papa.

"Oh, my, you have grown so much since you were 8," his mother said. "I hope this new robe I made you will last you all year."

As always, they walked over to the park across from the temple and sat down.

"Mama, Papa, there is something I do not understand," Samu-el explained as soon as they got settled on a big rug they could all sit on.

Samu-el pulled his knees up, rested his chin on them, and looked down at his toes.

"If you start twisting your toes," his papa said with a twinkle in his eye, "we know you are really worried about something."

"Why did you give me away?"

"Oh, Son," Hannah said. "We always loved you and always will. Before you were born, I ded-ica-ted you to God who loves you even more."

"What does that word mean—ded-ica-ted?"

Book 2: Samuel

"It means you are going to live for God your whole life. Everything you do will be for God. You will worship him every day, you will teach people God's laws every day, and you will love everyone as God loves everyone every day."

"Then I will become a priest one day?"

"Yes, when you are 30 years old, you will become a priest."

THINK AND DO

1. Have you thought about what you want to be when you grow up? Is it a fireman or a nurse or an animal doctor? What do you want to do?

2. How can you start while you are a child to maybe do a little bit of that kind of work you want to do when grown?

Book 2: Samuel

10 ~ The Voice

Samu-el was now 12 years old.

"I have been with you 9 years now, Grandfather," Samu-el said while eating his evening meal with High Priest Eli in his house.

"Yes, it has been a long time since I told your mother she would have you. God hasn't spoken to me in a long time. My eyes are getting dim. My thoughts of God seem to be getting dim too."

Eli sighed. "Well, I want you to go next door and sleep in the temple tonight. But sleep lightly. You must watch the golden candle sticks to make sure the fire does not go out on them during the night."

"Oh, Grandfather Eli. Really? You trust me to do that all night?" Samu-el said, his eyes lighting up and sparkling. "Oh, Grandfather! I will go right now."

"You must finish your dinner, then guide me to my bedroom. I can hardly see anything anymore.

An hour later, Samu-el was in the temple with his mat. Everyone else had left and gone home. He was all alone in

Book 2: Samuel

the temple, but he was not afraid because the golden candle sticks were bright.

He watched the flames dance until he became sleepy and fell asleep.

"Samu-el."

Samu-el wakened and sat up. He looked around for Eli. Eli was not there. No one was there. He left the temple and rushed next door to the high priest's house.

"Did you call me?" he asked when he got to Eli's bedroom.

The old man sat up in bed. "No, I didn't call you. Go back to your cot."

Samu-el rushed back to the temple so it would not be left un-attend-ed very long. He watched the flames on the golden candle sticks until he fell asleep again.

"Samu-el."

Samu-el wakened and sat up a 2nd time. He looked around for Eli. Eli was not there. No one was there. He left the temple and rushed next door to the high priest's house.

"Did you call me?" he asked when he got to Eli's bedroom.

The old man sat up in bed. "No, I didn't call you. Go back to your cot."

Book 2: Samuel

Samu-el rushed back to the temple so it would not be left un-attend-ed very long. He watched the flames on the golden candle sticks until he fell asleep again.

"Samu-el."

For a 3rd time, Samu-el could not see who was calling him and rushed back next door to Eli. This time, Eli sat all the way up in bed and pulled his feet around to the floor.

He motioned for Samu-el to come to him. Samu-el stood before the old man and Eli put his hands on the boy's shoulders. He was quiet for a moment.

"It is God," he said. "God is calling you. I have not heard God in a long time. It seems he wants you to take my place. Go back to your cot. He will call again. When he does, say, "Speak, Lord. I am your servant and I hear you."

"Yes, Grandfather."

"And, Samu-el, this is good."

Samu-el went back to his cot in the temple. He made up his mind he would not fall asleep again. But, as he watched the flames of the golden candle sticks, he fell asleep once more.

"Samu-el."

Book 2: Samuel

The boy sat up in his bed, stood, and looked around.

Then God told Samu-el everything he wanted him to say and do. Samu-el listened to every word God told him, and obeyed what God told him to do.

―――――

Many years passed after that. When Samu-el grew up, he became the judge over the whole Israel-ite kingdom. He taught his people and led them to face their enemies and do what was right. He even ap-pointed two kings.

The little fright-ened boy who was taken to the temple when he was only 3 years old grew up to be a mighty man of God.

Book 2: Samuel

THINK & DO

1. God does not speak directly to people any more. He hasn't for 2000 years. That's because everything he wants us to know has been written down in the Bible.

Do you want God to talk to you? He talks to you every time you read the Bible. Do you have a Bible of your very own? If not, ask the person reading to you or another grownup in your home if you can have a Bible of your own.

The Bible is divided into two parts: The Old Testa-ment written for Jews, and the New Testa-ment written for Christians. Start reading in the New

Testament. The first 4 mini-books of the New Testament are the life of Jesus Christ. Read it for yourself and let God tell you how much he loves you.

Especially read John 3:16, the 4th mini-book of the New Testament. It says,

"For God so loved the world, He gave His only begotten Son, so that whoever believes in him shall not perish but have eternal life."

And, even though you are a child, God loves you just as much as he did little Samu-el long, long ago.

Book 2: Samuel

Thank You

Thanks for reading my book! I'm so honored that you chose to spend your precious time with my characters and entrusted me to your child. You are appreciated.

I'm an independent author who relies on my readers to help spread the word about stories you enjoy. Would you take a few minutes to let your friends know on Facebook, Pinterest... wherever you hang out online?

Also, each honest review at online retailers means a lot to me and helps other readers know if this is a book they might enjoy.

I welcome contact from readers. At my website (below), you can do so. You can also sign up for my monthly newsletter (below) to be notified of new releases, half-price print books, and 99c ebooks.

A Child's Kids in the Bible

Buy Your Next Child's Book Now

Check out what they are about and get an international buy link.

A CHILD'S LIFE OF CHRIST Series of 8 books
http://bit.ly/ChildsLifeOfChristSet

A CHILD'S BIBLE HEROES Series of 10 books
http://bit.ly/ChildBibleHeroes

A CHILD'S BIBLE KIDS Series of 8 books
http://bit.ly/bible-kids

A CHILD'S BIBLE LADIES series of 10 books
http://bit.ly/2qmtwaA

OLD OLD STORY SET TO OLD OLD TUNES
http://bit.ly/BibleSongBook

FUN WITH BIBLE NUMBERS: 525 Problems
http://bit.ly/FunBibleNumbers

BIBLE PUZZLES FOR YOUNG & OLD
http://bit.ly/BiblePuzzlesYoungOld

Book 2: Samuel

About the Author

When the author was 17 some 60 years ago, she began writing her series of eight books called They Met Jesus. When she was 60, she completed it. It is now in child's form as A CHILD'S LIFE OF CHRIST.

Her four different series of children's books are most popular among grandparents and homeschoolers. But they are popular with children around the world. Her many novels and information books are popular with grownups.

Katheryn Maddox Haddad grew up in the north and now lives in Arizona where she doesn't have to shovel sunshine. She basks in 100-degree weather with palm trees, cacti, and a computer with most of the letters worn off.

Her newspaper column appeared for several years in newspapers in Texas and North Carolina – "Little Known Facts about the Bible."

She spends half her day writing, and the other half teaching English over the internet worldwide using the Bible as textbook. Students she has converted to Christianity are hiding all over the Middle East. "They are my heroes," she declares.

Each morning she sends out an inspirational scripture thought to over 30,000 people worldwide.

She is a member of Christian Writers of the West, American Christian Fiction Writers, Historical Novel Society, and the Phoenix Screen Writers Association.

Connect with the Author

Website: https://inspirationsbykatheryn.com

Facebook: https://bit.ly/FacebooksKatherynMaddoxHaddad

Linkedin: http://bit.ly/KatherynLinkedin

Twitter: https://twitter.com/KatherynHaddad

Pinterest: https://www.pinterest.com/haddad1940/

Goodreads: https://www.goodreads.com/katherynmaddoxhaddad

Book 2: Samuel

Get a Free Book

Sign up for Katheryn's monthly newsletter with half-price books for the whole family and insider tips on what's coming next.   http://bit.ly/katheryn

Join My Dream Team

Members get the first peek at my newest book and have fun offering me advice sometimes. I have a point system of rewards for helping me get the word out. Check it out here: http://bit.ly/KatherynsDreamTeam

A Child's Kids in the Bible

www.ingramcontent.com/pod-product-compliance
Lightning Source LLC
Chambersburg PA
CBHW071537080526
44588CB00011B/1703